PRESENTED TO

Stories for a Mom's Heart

OTHER BOOKS COMPILED
by ALICE GRAY

STORIES FOR THE HEART

MORE STORIES FOR THE HEART

CHRISTMAS STORIES FOR THE HEART

STORIES FOR THE FAMILY'S HEART

STORIES FOR A WOMAN'S HEART

STORIES FOR A MAN'S HEART

STORIES FOR A TEEN'S HEART

STORIES FOR A FAITHFUL HEART

STORIES FOR A DAD'S HEART

KEEPSAKES FOR THE HEART — MOTHERS

KEEPSAKES FOR THE HEART — FRIENDSHIP

KEEPSAKES FOR THE HEART — LOVE

KEEPSAKES FOR THE HEART — FAITH

(*Keepsakes for the Heart* is an elegant gift collection that includes a
hardbound book with full-color artwork, complementary bookmark,
note cards, and a charming box for keepsakes.)

Stories for a Mom's Heart

COMPILED *by* ALICE GRAY

Multnomah Publishers Sisters, Oregon

We have done our best to diligently seek reprint permission and provide accurate source attribution for all selections used in this book. However, if any attribution be found to be incorrect or lacking the proper permission license, the publisher welcomes notification and written documentation supporting corrections for subsequent printings. If you are, or know of, the proper copyright holder for any such story in this book, please contact us and we will properly credit and reimburse the contributor. We gratefully acknowledge the cooperation of other publishers and individuals for granting permission to use their material in this book.

Please see the bibliography at the back of the book for complete attributions for this material.

STORIES FOR A MOM'S HEART
published by Multnomah Publishers, Inc.

© 2000 by Multnomah Publishers, Inc.
International Standard Book Number: 1-57673-692-X

Photographs by David Bailey Photography
Design by the Office of Bill Chiaravalle

Scripture quotations are from:
The Holy Bible, New International Version (NIV)
© 1973, 1984 by International Bible Society,
used by permission of Zondervan Publishing House
The Living Bible (TLB)
© 1971. Used by permission of Tyndale House Publishers, Inc.
All rights reserved.

Multnomah is a trademark of Multnomah Publishers, Inc.,
and is registered in the U.S. Patent and Trademark Office.
The colophon is a trademark of Multnomah Publishers, Inc.

Printed in the United States of America

For information:
MULTNOMAH PUBLISHERS, INC. • P.O. BOX 1720 • SISTERS, OR 97759

Library of Congress Cataloging-in Publication Data
Stories for a mom's heart/compiled by Alice Gray.
    p.cm.
    ISBN 1-57673-692-X
    1. Mothers—Religious life—Anecdotes. 2. Mothers—Conduct of life—
    Anecdotes   I. Gray, Alice, 1939-
    BV4529.18.S76 2000
    242'.6431—dc21

                                                            99-050935

00 01 02 03 04 05 06 — 10 9 8 7 6 5 4 3 2 1 0

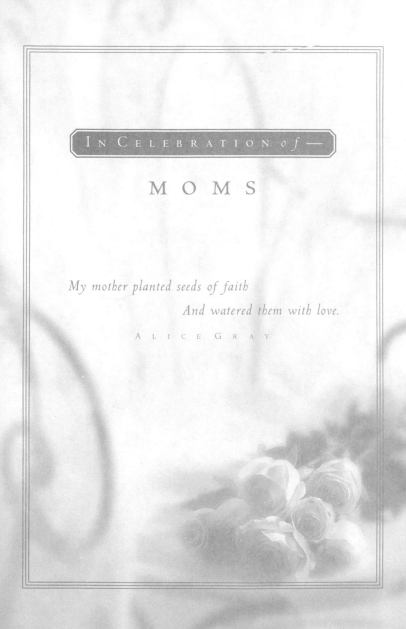

In Celebration of —

MOMS

My mother planted seeds of faith
And watered them with love.

ALICE GRAY

CONTENTS

A TRIBUTE TO MOMS

I   F O U N D   Y O U   T H E R E

Kathi Kingma

I held on to your hand across streets, over hills, through the valleys. Though the wind blew, though I tripped, you never let me fall. Sometimes I didn't look all the way up to see your face, but I saw your hand. It was twice as big as mine. I tried to take big steps like you, to be like you, but I still had to take two for each of yours. When my legs got tired, you carried me. It was fun to see everything from up high where I didn't have to try so hard to keep up. I always felt safe with my mom. As long as you were there, I know things would be okay. When I was scared, I reached for your hand and found you there.

When I got older, I wanted to walk more on my own. I learned to navigate the path of life, over hills and through the valleys. I glimpsed at freedom and independence. You still walked beside me and helped me get up when I fell.

Now I am grown up. My stride equals yours. I look you in the eyes and I do not tire as we walk. But you have not changed. You are still there as support, as counsel, as unchanging love. Because of you, a little one will rush up to me someday. Full of adventure, she'll walk with me across streets, over hills and through valleys. She'll take steps trying to make them big like mine. She'll trip and I'll catch her. She'll reach up for my hand and find me there.

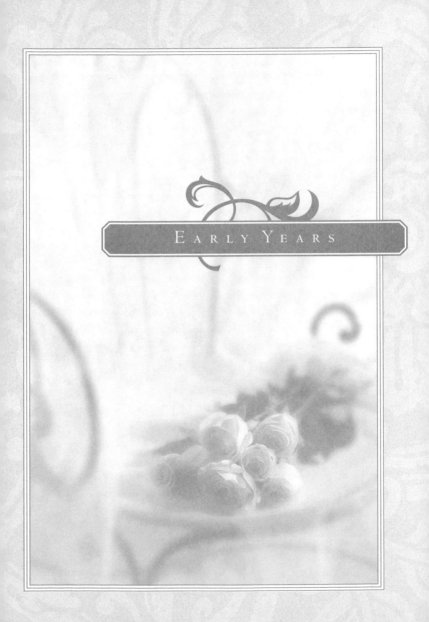

EARLY YEARS

A   M O T H E R ' S   L E T T E R   T O   A   S O N
S T A R T I N G   K I N D E R G A R T E N
Rebecca Christian

Dear George,

 When your big brother and your little dog and I walked you up to school today, you had no idea how I was feeling.

You were so excited, you had packed and unpacked the washable markers and safety scissors in your backpack a dozen times.

I am really going to miss those lazy mornings when we waved your brother and sister off to school. I'd settle in with my coffee and newspaper, handing you the comics to color while you watched *Sesame Street.*

Because you are my youngest, I had learned a few things by the time you came along. I found out that the seemingly endless days of babyhood are gone like lightning. I blinked, and your older siblings were setting off for school as eagerly as you did this morning.

I was one of the lucky ones; I could choose whether to work or not. By the time it was your turn, the glittering prizes of career advancement and a double income had lost their luster. A splash in the puddles with you in your bright red boots or "just one more" rereading of your favorite book, *Frog and Toad Are Friends,* meant more.

You didn't go to preschool and I'm not exactly Maria Montessori. I hope that doesn't hold you back. You learned numbers by helping me count the soda cans we returned to the store. (You could usually charm me into letting you pick out a treat with the money we got back.)

I'm not up on the Palmer method, but you do a fine job of writing your name on the sidewalk in chalk, in capitals to make it look more important. And somehow you caught on to the nuances of language. Just the other day, you asked me why I always call you "honey" when we're reading stories and "Bud" when you're helping with the chores. My explanation of the difference between a cuddly mood and a matey one seemed to satisfy you.

I have to admit that in my mind's eye, an image of myself while you're in school has developed. I see myself updating all the photo albums and starting that novel I always wanted to write. As the summer wound down and more frequent quarrels erupted between you and your siblings, I was looking forward to today.

And then this morning, I walked you up the steep hill to your classroom with a picture of the president on one wall and of Bambi on the opposite. You found the coat hook with your name above it right away, and you gave me one of your characteristically fierce, too-tight hugs. This time you were ready to let go before I was.

Maybe someday you will deliver a kindergartner with your own wide-set eyes and sudden grin to the first day of school. When you turn at the door to wave good-bye, he or she will be too deep in conversation with a new friend to notice. Even as you smile, you'll feel something warm on your cheek...

And then, you'll know.

Love, Mom

THIS IS A HOME WHERE CHILDREN LIVE

Judith Bond

You may not find things all in place,
Friend, when you enter here.
But, we're a home where children live,
We hold them very dear.
And you may find small fingerprints
And smudges on the wall.
When the kids are gone, we'll clean them up,
Right now we're playing ball.
For there's one thing of which we're sure,
These children are on loan.
One day they're always underfoot,
Next thing you know, they're gone.
That's when we'll have a well kept house,
When they're off on their own.
Right now, this is where children live,
a loved and lived in home.

TWICE BLESSED
Kathryn Lay

*O*n the day my husband and I learned of our imminent adoption of our nine-month-old daughter, we joyously took our closest friends out to dinner in celebration.

While we laughed and talked at the restaurant, telling them of what we knew about our soon-to-arrive and much-prayed-for daughter, I became aware that the older couple in the booth behind us laughed as we did and nodded knowingly as we voiced our excitement and nervousness.

After ten years of infertility, of prayers, and eight months of parenting classes and paperwork and home studies—we were full of joy at the good news. It bubbled over as we talked and planned in the restaurant.

When the couple behind us left their booth, they paused at our table.

"Congratulations," the woman said, patting my shoulder.

"Thank you," I said, grateful that they weren't angry at our loudness.

She leaned closer and said, "I have several children of my own. I have a granddaughter who was adopted by someone not long ago.

I've never seen her. Hearing your excitement, I feel in my heart that somewhere she is loved and well taken care of by a family like you."

Patting my shoulder once more, she whispered, "I'll pray for you and your baby."

At a time when we were blessed and overflowing with joy, God put us in a place where we could be a blessing and comfort to another. I pray for that grandmother, that God will continue to give her peace and comfort for the granddaughter she wonders about. And I know that my husband and I were in her prayers that night.

A mother's arms are made of tenderness,
and children sleep soundly in them.
— *Victor Hugo*

NEW MOTHERHOOD

*E*very mother practices the ritual of counting tiny fingers and toes, cupping the small head in one's hand, stroking gossamer hair, and trying to determine just whose side of the family is responsible for those ears and that nose—all rites of new motherhood, both private and public, that mark the beginning of a whole new world.

Pamela Scurry

FROM CRADLE AND ALL

B R E A K F A S T   W I T H   T H E
P O L A R   B E A R S
Allison Harms

I went to college when my son went to kindergarten. I had more homework than he did, but we shared the field trips— I chaperoned his class to the fire station and the farm and he joined my class for a couple of fossil hunts and glacier hikes. Once, for one of my biology classes, I was required to visit the zoo on my own sometime during the fall term. I put if off for weeks, waiting for Indian Summer, busy with our new back-to-school schedules. Finally I realized that the end of the term was approaching and I hadn't completed the assignment. I chose a day for the zoo excursion. Of course my son came along too.

It wasn't a typical day at the zoo. The late fall, too early winter weather kept it deserted except for my son and me. Even the animals seemed scarce. Clouds closed down the sky and spat rain that felt like ice needles. Damp gusts eddied around our legs, catching up shredded leaves, paper bags, candy wrappers and peanut shells in a whirlpool of compost at the corner of the reptile house. Only a few eerie fluorescent lights glowed inside. We walked on. The fountains were drained, the garden beds left desolate, the boulevards

empty. Ducks huddled together on the lee side of the lake, heads tucked under their wings. Tiny waves smacked the shore. As we walked, the wind filled then flattened our coats against our bodies.

Our footfalls on the paved walk alerted the gazelles at their grazing. A herd of sharp heads, ears, and horns poised like a ballet troupe on tiptoe as we passed. In the distance, we heard the elephant's bugle. The lion's amber eyes followed us; his tufted tail flicked once against the floor. The surface of the hippopotamus's pool winked and the matron lifted her bobbin snout and blinked her liquid eye. The giraffe cocked his head and stared gravely.

We stopped to watch the polar bears. They marched with cool, lumbering strides but their gait was comically bow-legged and pigeon-toed. They had overgrown puppies' paws fringed with curved, black claws. Muzzles up, they sniffed the air, swinging their too small, bullet heads from side-to-side and snorting dragon-curls of steam against the cement sky. The scent of snow was as comforting to them as a sunbath for a house cat.

Their keeper came around the corner wearing rubber boots and swinging two red buckets. At their first sight of him, the bears began to plunge into the pool with the rumbling chaos of boulders in an avalanche. They clambered out again, water streaming from their bodies like snowmelt from the mountains.

The keeper walked over to where my son and I stood.

"Good morning," we said to each other. I asked him what was in the buckets.

"Mackerel and watermelon."

"Is that what bears eat for breakfast?" my son asked.

"Yep," the keeper answered. Then bending down to my son's height, he said, "Like to help me feed the bears?"

"Wow! Can I, Mom?"

And so we did, tossing dark wedges of fish and mottled melon rinds into winter's first breath of snow.

Too soon it was time to leave. My son was tired so I carried him in my arms, his hood pulled over his ears, his face pressed into my shoulder. I smiled to myself as I thought of how often the "have tos" in my life turned into "get tos": I had to go to the zoo; I got to spend the day with my son *and* feed breakfast to the polar bears. Doing what's right has rewards of its own. But I could remember so many times when I'd fulfilled an obligation or followed through on a promise even when it cost me to keep it, and something new had opened up for me: a relationship, a skill, an unforgettable moment. And even on the blustery November day, I knew that the memory of our simple, unexpected experience—breakfast with the polar bears—would warm us deep down inside every time we remembered it.

ALONE TIME FOR MOM

Crystal Kirgiss

FROM *DETROIT LAKES TRIBUNE*

All I needed this morning was a half-hour alone, thirty minutes of peace and quiet to help preserve my sanity. No mom-do-this, mom-I-need-that, mom-he-hit-me, mom-I-spilled-juice-on-the-couch.

Just me, a hot Calgon bath, and nothingness.

I shouldn't dream so big.

After getting the two oldest off to school, I settled the youngest in front of Barney and said, "Honey, listen closely. Your mommy is going to crack. She's losing her marbles. She's teetering on the edge of permanent personality damage. This is because she has children. Are you following me so far?"

He nodded absently while singing, "Barney is a dinosaur in our imagination. . . ."

"Good. Now, if you want to be a good little boy, you'll sit right here and watch Barney while Mommy takes a nice, hot, quiet, peaceful, take-me-away bath. I don't want you to bother me. I want you to leave me alone. For 30 minutes, I don't want to see you or hear you. Got it?"

Nod.

"Good morning, boys and girls..." I heard the purple wonder say.

I headed to the bathroom with my fingers crossed.

I watched the water fill the tub. I watched the mirror and window steam up. I watched the water turn blue from my bath beads. I got in.

I heard a knock on the door.

"Mom? Mom? Are you in there, Mom?!"

I learned long ago that ignoring my children does not make them go away.

"Yes, I'm in here. What do you want?"

There was a long pause while the child tried to decide what he wanted.

"Um...can I have a snack?"

"You just had breakfast! Can't you wait a few minutes?"

"No, I'm dying! I need a snack right now!"

"Fine. You can have a box of raisins."

I heard him pad off to the kitchen, listened as he pushed chairs and stools around trying to reach the raisin shelf, felt the floor vibrate when he jumped off the counter, and heard him run back to the TV room.

"Hi, Susie! Can you tell me what color the grass is...?"

Knock, knock, knock.

"Mom? Mom? Are you in there, Mom?!"

Sigh. "Yes, I'm still in here. What do you need now?"

Pause. "Um...I need to take a bath, too."

Right.

"Honey, can't you wait until I'm done?"

The door opened just a crack.

"No, I really need to take one now. I'm dirty."

"You're always dirty! Since when do you care?"

The door opened all the way.

"I really need to take a bath, Mom."

"No, you don't. Go away."

He stood in the middle of the bathroom and started taking off his pajamas.

"I'll just get in with you and take a bath, too."

"No! You will not get in with me and take a bath! I want to take my own bath! I want you to go away and leave me alone!" I began to sound like the three-year-old with whom I was arguing.

He climbed onto the edge of the tub, balancing carefully, and said, "I'll just get in *with* you, okay, Mom?"

I started to shriek, "No! That is not okay! I want my own bath,

all by myself! I don't want to share! I want to be alone!"

He thought for a moment and said, "Okay. I'll just sit here and you can read me a book. I won't get in, Mom, until you're done." He flashed me a knock-down charming smile.

So I spent my morning-alone-time reading *One Fish, Two Fish* to a naked three-year-old who sat on the edge of the tub with his chin resting on his knees, arms wrapped around his bent legs, slight smile on his face.

Why fight it? It won't be long before I have all the alone-time I want. And then I'll probably feel bad about not having any more together-time.

Making the decision to have a child—it's momentous.
It is to decide forever to have your heart
go walking around outside your body.
—*Elizabeth Stone*

FUTURE HOPE

"For I know the plans I have for you,"

*declares the L*ORD,

"plans to prosper you and not to harm you,

and to give you hope and a future."

JEREMIAH 29:11

LOVE LETTERS TO MY UNBORN CHILD
Judith Hayes

*I*t was a balmy summer day in late July. I had been feeling rather queasy and nauseated, so I decided to see my doctor.

"Mrs. Hayes, I'm happy to tell you that you are ten weeks pregnant," my doctor announced. I couldn't believe my ears. It was a dream come true.

My husband and I were young and had been married for only a year. We were working hard to build a happy life together. The news that we were expecting a baby was exciting and scary.

In my youthful enthusiasm I decided to write "love letters" to our baby to express my feelings of expectancy and joy. Little did I know just how valuable those love letters would be in years to come.

August 1971: Oh, my darling baby, can you feel the love I have for you while you are so small and living in the quiet world inside my body? Your daddy and I want the world to be perfect for you with no hate, no wars, no pollution. I can't wait to hold you in my arms in just six months! I love you, and Daddy loves you but he can't feel you yet.

September 1971: I am four months pregnant and am feeling better. I can tell you are growing, and I hope you are well and

comfortable. I've been taking vitamins and eating healthy foods for you. Thank goodness my morning sickness is gone. I think about you all the time.

October 1971: Oh, these melancholy moods. I cry so often over so little. Sometimes I feel very alone, and then I remember you are growing inside of me. I feel you stirring, now tumbling and turning and pushing. It's never the same. Your movements always bring me so much joy!

November 1971: I am feeling much better now that my fatigue and nausea have passed. The intense heat of summer is over. The weather is lovely, crisp and breezy. I feel your movements often now. Constant punching and kicking. What elation to know you are alive and well. Last week Daddy and I heard your strong heartbeat at the doctor's office.

February 2, 1972 at 11:06 P.M.: You were born! We named you Sasha. It was a long, hard twenty-two hour labor, and your daddy helped me relax and stay calm. We are so happy to see you, to hold you, and to greet you. Welcome, our firstborn child. We love you so much!

Sasha was soon one year old and cautiously toddling all over the house. Then she was riding ponies and swinging in the sunshine

at the park. Our little blue-eyed beauty entered kindergarten and grew into a bright and strong-willed little girl. The years passed so quickly that my husband and I joked that we put our five-year-old daughter to bed one night and she woke up the next morning as a teenager.

Those few years of adolescence and rebellion were not easy. There were times my beautiful yet angry teenager would dig her feet into the ground and yell. "You never loved me! You don't care about me or want me to be happy!"

Her harsh words cut at my heart. What could I have done wrong?

After one of my daughter's angry outbursts, I suddenly remembered the little box of love letters tucked away in my bedroom closet. I found them and quietly placed them on her bed, hoping she would read them. A few days later, she appeared before me with tears in her eyes.

"Mom, I never knew just how much you truly loved me—even before I was born!" she said. "How could you love me without knowing me? You loved me unconditionally!" That very precious moment became a bond of unity that still exists between us today. Those dusty old love letters melted away the anger and rebellion she had been feeling.

TO MY GROWN-UP SON

Author unknown

My hands were busy through the day;
I didn't have much time to play
The little games you asked me to—
I didn't have much time for you.
I'd wash your clothes, I'd sew and cook;
But when you'd bring your picture book
And ask me please to share your fun,
I'd say: "A little later, son."
I'd tuck you in all safe at night,
And hear your prayers, turn out the light,
Then tip-toe softly to the door....
I wish I'd stayed a minute more.
For life is short, the years rush past....
A little boy grows up so fast.

No longer is he at your side,
His precious secrets to confide.
The picture books are put away;
There are no longer games to play.
No good-night kiss, no prayers to hear—
That all belongs to yesteryear.
My hands, once busy, now are still.
The days are long and hard to fill.
I wish I could go back and do
The little things you asked me to.

The most glorious sight that one ever sees beneath the
stars is the sight of worthy motherhood.
— George W. Truett

GROWING UP

WHAT A MOTHER SAYS
Robin Jones Gunn

FROM *MOTHERING BY HEART*

Oh, let me hold her!

How's my little angel?

Hush, baby girl.

Aren't you sleepy yet?

It's okay. Don't cry.

No, no. Don't touch.

Come to Mommy.

Take that out of your mouth. Yucky!

That's not for you.

You don't need that anymore.

You're a big girl now.

Tell Mommy if you need to go potty, okay?

Don't get into your brother's things.

Go to your room.

No, you may not.

I just brought you a drink of water.

Get back in bed.

Pick up your toys.

Don't play inside the clothes rack.
Can you draw a picture for Grandma?
Hold still.
Can you remember to bring it home tomorrow?
I'm sure she still wants to be your friend.
Did you practice?
Try looking under your bed.
Go wash your hands.
You're not old enough yet.
You'll have to ask your father.
Where was it when you last saw it?
Stop teasing your brother.
Go clean your room. Come set the table.
Don't bite your nails.
Did you do your homework?
Get off the phone. Eat your vegetables.
You're responsible to keep track of your own things.
Did you tell me it was this Saturday?
Sure—if you want to use your own money.
Tell her you'll call her back.
Try on a bigger size.
There's a boy on the phone for you.
You may not wear that to school.

Be back by your curfew.

I did not say it was okay.

Come straight home.

No, I need the car this afternoon.

Are you coming home this weekend? Next weekend?

What do you know about him?

Have you thought this through?

I ordered them because I thought you'd appreciate them.

But pink used to be your favorite color.

Whatever you want. It's up to you.

Don't sit on your veil.

Call us when you get there. Don't slip on the rice.

Good-bye, honey.

*I have no greater joy than to hear
that my children walk in truth.*

— 3 JOHN 1:4

NO MORE OATMEAL KISSES

Erma Bombeck

FROM *FOREVER, ERMA*

A young mother writes: "I know you've written before about the empty-nest syndrome, that lonely period after the children are grown and gone. Right now I'm up to my eyeballs in laundry and muddy boots. The baby is teething; the boys are fighting. My husband just called and said to eat without him, and I fell off my diet. Lay it on me again, will you?"

OK. One of these days, you'll shout, "Why don't you kids grow up and act your age!" And they will. Or, "You guys get outside and find yourselves something to do...and don't slam the door!" And they won't.

You'll straighten up the boys' bedroom neat and tidy: bumper stickers discarded, bedspread tucked and smooth, toys displayed on the shelves. Hangers in the closet. Animals caged. And you'll say out loud, "Now I want it to stay this way." And it will.

You'll prepare a perfect dinner with a salad that hasn't been picked to death and a cake with no finger traces in the icing, and you'll say, "Now, there's a meal for company." And you'll eat it alone.

You'll say, "I want complete privacy on the phone. No dancing

around. No demolition crews. Silence! Do you hear?" And you'll have it.

No more plastic tablecloths stained with spaghetti. No more bedspreads to protect the sofa from damp bottoms. No more gates to stumble over at the top of the basement steps. No more clothes-pins under the sofa. No more playpens to arrange a room around.

No more anxious nights under a vaporizer tent. No more sand on the sheets or Popeye movies in the bathroom. No more iron-on patches, rubber bands for ponytails, tight boots or wet knotted shoestrings.

Imagine. A lipstick with a point on it. No baby-sitter for New Year's Eve. Washing only once a week. Seeing a steak that isn't ground. Having your teeth cleaned without a baby on your lap.

No PTA meetings. No car pools. No blaring radios. No one washing her hair at 11 o'clock at night. Having your own roll of Scotch tape.

Think about it. No more Christmas presents out of toothpicks and library paste. No more sloppy oatmeal kisses. No more tooth fairy. No more giggles in the dark. No knees to heal, no responsibility.

Only a voice crying, "Why don't you grow up?" and the silence echoing, "I did."

*I am not in any doubt as to how
my own Christian experience began.
The altar before which I knelt
first was my mother's knee.*
—*L. D. Weatherhead*

SEEING EACH OTHER IN
A DIFFERENT LIGHT
Susan Manegold
FROM *WOMEN'S WORLD MAGAZINE*

When my daughters were little, we loved to spend time together talking or watching TV. But by the time Lauren and Carly were teens, they preferred being in their own rooms, talking on the phone or listening to music, to being with me—or even each other.

I knew it was just a part of their growing up, but while I wanted my daughters to be independent, I also wanted them to be close, and a part of me missed the days when we'd all curl up on the couch with a bowl of popcorn.

Then one windy night while their dad was working, the lights went out. "Cool!" I heard Carly, thirteen, call from her room.

"I hate this!" Lauren, eighteen, cried.

Grabbing candles and a flashlight, I headed for the girls' rooms. Lauren's was already filled with the cozy glow of candlelight, so Carly and I filed in, and soon we were all snuggled on Lauren's bed.

Carly was excited, but Lauren pouted when Carly suggested, "Let's tell stories." As Carly began to talk about school and her

friends, however, Lauren's pout disappeared. She snuggled closer to Carly, and soon they were giggling just like they had when they were younger.

I could tell from the sparkle in Carly's eyes that she knew the darkness had brought us a gift, but I wondered if Lauren felt the same way. Suddenly, Lauren's phone rang. "Yeah, our power is out too," she told her friend. "But I'll have to call you back. I'm hanging out with my mom and my sister."

She knows it too! I thought. And after she hung up, she offered, "Let's sing songs." Tears filled my eyes.

A short while later, the power came back on. "Oh no!" the girls groaned. But since then, we've all felt closer. We hug more, and the girls don't tease each other as much. Some nights we just sit and talk. The power outage didn't just leave us in the dark; it gave us the opportunity to see each other in a different light.

*No nation ever had a better friend than the
mother who taught her children to pray.*

LIFE TREASURES

I long to put the experience of fifty years at once into your young lives, to give you at once the key of that treasure chamber every gem of which has cost me tears and struggles and prayers, but you must work for these inward treasures yourselves.

Harriet Beecher Stowe

S H E ' S   S E V E N T E E N
Gloria Gaither

FROM *LET'S MAKE A MEMORY*

*T*he first day of school didn't start until one o'clock, so there was plenty of time for breakfast at McDonald's and shopping for the supplies that had been listed in the *Times-Tribune* the Wednesday before. You reminded us to go to McDonald's for breakfast. "We've always gone there on the first day of school," you said. Something hard to label stirred inside me when you said it. Perhaps it was pride—pride that you still found joy in our crazy little tradition; or perhaps it was pleasure—pleasure in knowing that you still choose to be with our family when you have your "druthers." But there was a certain sadness, too, and I couldn't stop the knowing this was your last first day of school.

You came down the stairs that morning all neat and well-groomed, the healthy glow of your summer tan and freckles still showing through your make-up, your sun-bleached hair carefully arranged. "Hi, Mom!" you said, and your grin showed your straight, white teeth. No more orthodontist appointments, I thought, and no more broken glasses to glue before school. Contacts and braces had sure been worth it.

"I've got to have my senior pictures taken tomorrow after school, Mom. Can I use the car?"

"As far as I know," I answered, then reminded you of your promise to take your sister to get her hair trimmed at three o'clock that afternoon. Your driver's license had come in handy, too.

By then Amy and Benjy were ready, and we all piled into the car and drove to McDonald's. As we ate, we talked about other first days—the first day of kindergarten, their first day of junior high, and that scary first day in the big new high school. You all interrupted each other with stories of embarrassing moments, awards, friendships, and fright.

After we had eaten, we hurried to buy notebook paper and compasses before I dropped you all at school—first Amy and Benjy at the middle school, then you. "Bye, Mom," you said as you scooted across the seat. Then you stopped a moment and looked back over your shoulder. "And, Mom...thanks." It was the remnant of a kiss good-bye. It was the hesitancy of a little girl in ringlets beginning kindergarten. It was the anticipation of a young woman confident of her direction—these were all there in that gesture.

"I love you," was all I answered, but I had hoped that somehow you could hear with your heart the rest of the words that were going through my mind—words that told you how special you are to us;

words that would let you know how rich your father and I have been because you came into our lives; words that tell you how much we believe in you, hope for you, pray for you, thank God for you. As the school doors closed behind you and you disappeared into the corridor, I wanted so to holler after you: *"Wait!* We have so much yet to do. We've never been to Hawaii. We've never taken a cruise. That book of poetry we wrote together isn't published yet. And what about the day we were going to spend at the cabin just being still and reading? Or the writers' workshop we planned to attend together in Illinois? You can't go yet. . . . *Wait!"*

But I knew you couldn't wait, and that we could never keep you by calling a halt to your progress. You had promises to keep. And so, though I knew this was a last first, I also somehow knew that it was a first in a whole lifetime of new beginnings...and I rejoiced!

&

No man is poor who had a godly mother.
— Abraham Lincoln

WHEN GROWN KIDS COME TO VISIT

Erma Bombeck

FROM *FOREVER, ERMA*

*I*n earlier days, I was a mother who made her kids pick up their rooms, make their own snacks and put their laundry in the utility room. Now when they come home, I put the rules aside. I am like a concierge looking for a big tip. I follow them around asking, "Are you hungry? Can I get you something? Do you have laundry?"

I eat when they want to eat, cook their favorite foods just before they tell me they are going out with friends and watch helplessly as they eat their way through a pound of baked ham at three in the afternoon.

On their visit, my life changes. I have no car. My washer is set at extra-large load and has two socks and a T-shirt in it. The phone rings constantly and is never for me.

At the end of their visits, we set aside a day, pack a lunch and head for the airport. It isn't until I return home that I sense how orderly my life has become. I enjoy the quiet. The TV tuner is res-

cued from the clothes hamper and is returned to its place on the coffee table. The empty milk and juice cartons are removed from the refrigerator. The wet towels are put in the washer. The bathroom is returned to health standards.

It is my world again. So why am I crying?

The heart of a mother is a deep abyss at the bottom of which you will always find forgiveness.
—*H o n o r é   d e   B a l z a c*

SILENT WORK

Nothing can compare in beauty, and wonder, and admirableness, and divinity itself, to the silent work in obscure dwellings of faithful women bringing their children to honor and virtue and piety.

Henry Ward Beecher

S O M E D A Y

Charles R. Swindoll

FROM *COME BEFORE WINTER*

*S*OMEDAY WHEN THE KIDS ARE GROWN, things are going to be a lot different. The garage won't be full of bikes, electric train tracks on plywood, sawhorses surrounded by chunks of two-by-fours, nails, a hammer and saw, unfinished "experimental projects," and the rabbit cage. I'll be able to park both cars neatly in just the right places, and never again stumble over skateboards, a pile of papers (saved for the school fund drive), or the bag of rabbit food—now split and spilled.

SOMEDAY WHEN THE KIDS ARE GROWN, the kitchen will be incredibly neat. The sink will be free of sticky dishes, the garbage disposal won't get choked on rubber bands or paper cups, the refrigerator won't be clogged with nine bottles of milk, and we won't lose the tops to jelly jars, catsup bottles, the peanut butter, the margarine, or the mustard. The water jar won't be put back empty, the ice trays won't be left out overnight, the blender won't stand for six hours coated with the remains of a midnight malt, and the honey will stay inside the container.

Someday when the kids are grown, my lovely wife will actually have time to get dressed leisurely. A long, hot bath (without three panic interruptions), time to do her nails (even toenails if she pleases!) without answering a dozen questions and reviewing spelling words, having had her hair done that afternoon without trying to squeeze it in between racing a sick dog to the vet and a trip to the orthodontist with a kid in a bad mood because she lost her headgear.

Someday when the kids are grown, the instrument called a "telephone" will actually be available. It won't look like it's growing from a teenager's ear. It will simply hang there...silently and amazingly available! It will be free of lipstick, human saliva, mayonnaise, corn chip crumbs, and toothpicks stuck in those little holes.

Someday when the kids are grown, I'll be able to see through the car windows. Fingerprints, tongue licks, sneaker footprints and dog tracks (nobody knows how) will be conspicuous by their absence. The back seat won't be a disaster area, we won't sit on jacks or crayons anymore, the tank will not always be somewhere between empty and fumes, and (glory to God!) I won't have to clean up dog messes another time.

SOMEDAY WHEN THE KIDS ARE GROWN, we will return to normal conversations. You know, just plain American talk. "Gross" won't punctuate every sentence seven times. "Yuk!" will not be heard. "Hurry up, I gotta go!" will not accompany the banging of fists on the bathroom door. "It's my turn" won't call for a referee. And a magazine article will be read in full without interruption, then discussed at length without mom and dad having to hide in the attic to finish the conversation.

SOMEDAY WHEN THE KIDS ARE GROWN, we won't run out of toilet tissue. My wife won't lose her keys. We won't forget to shut the refrigerator door. I won't have to dream up new ways of diverting attention from the gumball machine...or have to answer "Daddy, is it a sin that you're driving forty-seven in a thirty-mile-per-hour zone?"...or promise to kiss the rabbit goodnight...or wait up forever until they get home from dates...or have to take a number to get a word in at the supper table...or endure the pious pounding of one Keith Green just below the level of acute pain.

Yes, someday when the kids are grown, things are going to be a lot different. One by one they'll leave our nest, and the place will begin to resemble order and maybe even a touch of elegance. The

clink of china and silver will be heard on occasion. The crackling of the fireplace will echo through the hallway. The phone will be strangely silent. The house will be quiet...and calm...and always clean...and empty...and we'll spend our time not looking forward to Someday but looking back to Yesterday. And thinking, "Maybe we can baby-sit the grandkids and get some life back in this place for a change!"

The mother's heart is the child's school-room.
— Henry Ward Beecher

S E A S O N   O F   T H E   E M P T Y   N E S T
Joan Mills

*R*emember when the children built blanket tents to sleep in? And then scrambled by moonlight to their own beds, where they'd be safe from bears? And how proud and eager they were to be starting kindergarten? But only up to the minute they got there? And the time they packed cardboard suitcases in such a huff? "You won't see *us* again!" they hollered. Then they turned back at the end of the yard because they'd forgotten to go to the bathroom?

It's the same thing when they're twenty or twenty-two, starting to make their own way in the grownup world. Bravado, pangs, false starts and pitfalls. They're half in, half out. "Good-bye, good-bye! Don't worry, Mom!" They're back the first weekend to borrow the paint roller and a fuse and a broom. Prowling the attic, they seize on the quilt the dog ate and the terrible old sofa cushions that smell like dead mice. "Just what I need!" they cheer, loading the car.

"Good-bye, good-bye!" implying forever. But they show up without notice at suppertimes, sighing soulfully to see the familiar laden plates. They go away again, further secured by four bags of groceries, the electric frying pan and a cookbook.

They call home collect, but not as often as parents need to

hear. And their news makes fast-graying hair stand on end: "So he forgot to set the brake, and he says my car rolled three blocks backward down the hill before it was totaled!" "Simple case of last hired, first fired, no big deal. I sold the stereo, and..." "Mom! Everybody in the city has them! There's this roach stuff you put under the sink. It's..."

I gripped the phone with both hands in those days, wishing I could bribe my children back with everything they'd ever wanted— drum lessons, a junk-food charge account, anything. I struggled with an unbecoming urge to tell them once more about hot breakfasts and crossing streets and dry socks on wet days.

"I'm *so* impressed by how you cope!" I said instead.

The children scatter, and parents draw together, remembering sweet-shaped infants heavy in their arms, patched jeans, chicken pox, the night the accident happened, the rituals of Christmases and proms. With wistful pride and a feeling for the comic, they watch over their progeny from an effortfully kept distance. It is the season of the empty nest.

Slowly, slowly, there are changes. Something wonderful seems to hover then, faintly heard, glimpsed in illumined moments. Visiting the children, the parents are almost sure of it.

A son spreads a towel on the table and efficiently irons a per-

fect crease into his best pants. (*Ironing board,* his mother thinks, adding to a mental shopping list.) "I'm taking you to a French restaurant for dinner," the young man announces. "I've made reservations."

"Am I properly dressed?" his mother asks, suddenly shy. He walks her through city streets within the aura of his assurance. His arm lies lightly around her shoulders.

Or a daughter offers her honored guests the only two chairs she has and settles into a harem heap of floor pillows. She has raised plants from cuttings, framed a wall full of prints herself, spent three weekends refinishing the little dresser that glows in a square of sun.

Her parents regard her with astonished love. The room has been enchanted by her touch. "Everything's charming," they tell her honestly. "It's a real home."

Now? Is it *now?* Yes. The something wonderful descends. The generations smile at one another, as if exchanging congratulations. The children are no longer children. The parents are awed to discover adults.

It *is* wonderful, in ways my imagination had not begun to dream on. How could I have guessed—how could they?—that of my three, the shy one would pluck a dazzling array of competencies out of the air and turn up, chatting with total poise, on

TV shows? That the one who turned his adolescence into World War III would find his role in arduous, sensitive human service? Or that the unbookish, antic one, torment of his teachers, would evolve into a scholar, tolerating a student's poverty and writing into the night?

I hadn't suspected that my own young adults would be so ebulliently funny one minute, and so tellingly introspective the next; so open-hearted and unguarded. Or that growing up would inspire them to buy life insurance and three-piece suits and lend money to the siblings they'd once robbed of lollypops. Or that walking into their houses, I'd hear Mozart on the tape player and find books laid out for me to borrow.

Once, long ago, I waited nine months at a time to see who they would be, babes newly formed and wondrous. "Oh, *look!*" I said, and fell in love. Now my children are wondrously new to me in a different way. I am in love again.

My daughter and I freely share the complex world of our inner selves, and all the other worlds we know. Touched, I notice how her rhythms and gestures are reminding me of her grandmother's or mine. We are linked by unconscious mysteries and benignly watched by ghosts. I turn my head to gaze at her. She meets my look and smiles.

A son flies the width of the country for his one vacation in a whole long year. He follows me around the kitchen, tasting from the pots, handing down the dishes. We brown in the sun. Read books in silent synchrony. He jogs. I tend the flowers. We walk at the unfurled edge of great waves. We talk and talk, and later play cribbage past midnight. I'm utterly happy.

"But it's your vacation!" I remind him. "What shall we do that's special?"

"This," he says. "Exactly this."

When my children first ventured out and away, I felt they were in flight to outer space, following a curve of light and time to such unknowns that my heart would surely go faint with trying to follow. I thought this would be the end of parenting. Not what it is—the best part; the final, firmest bonding; the goal and the reward.

REPRINTED WITH PERMISSION OF
THE READER'S DIGEST ASSOCIATION, INC.

LOVE

THE BOBBY PINS
Linda Goodman

When I was seven years old, I overheard my mother tell one of her friends that the following day was to be her thirtieth birthday. Two things occurred to me when I heard that: one, I had never before realized that my mother had a birthday; and two, I could not recall her ever getting a birthday present.

Well, I could do something about that. I went into my bedroom, opened my piggy bank and took out all the money that was inside: five nickels. That represented five weeks' worth of my allowance. Then I walked to the little store around the corner from my house, and I told the proprietor, Mr. Sawyer, that I wanted to buy a birthday present for my mother.

He showed me everything in his store that could be had for a quarter. There were several ceramic figurines. My mother would have loved those, but she already had a house full of them and I was the one who had to dust them once a week. They definitely would not do. There were also some small boxes of candy. My mother was diabetic, so I knew they would not be appropriate.

The last thing Mr. Sawyer showed me was a package of bobby pins. My mother had beautiful long black hair, and twice a week she

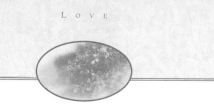

washed and pincurled it. When she took the pincurls down the next day, she looked just like a movie star with those long, dark curls cascading around her shoulders. So I decided those bobby pins would be the perfect gift for my mother. I gave Mr. Sawyer my five nickels, and he gave me the bobby pins.

I took the bobby pins home and wrapped them in a colorful sheet from the Sunday comics (there was no money left for wrapping paper). The next morning, I walked up to my mother and handed her that package and said, "Happy birthday, Momma!"

My mother sat there for a moment in stunned silence. Then, with tears in her eyes, she tore at that comic-strip wrapping. By the time she got to the bobby pins, she was sobbing.

"I'm sorry, Momma!" I apologized. "I didn't mean to make you cry. I just wanted you to have a happy birthday."

"Oh, honey, I am happy!" she told me. And I looked into her eyes, and I could see that she was smiling through her tears. "Why, do you know that this is the first birthday present that I have ever received in my entire life?" she exclaimed.

Then she kissed me on the cheek and said, "Thank you, honey." And she turned to my sister and said, "Lookee here! Linda got me a birthday present!" And she turned to my father and said, *"Lookee here! Linda got me a birthday present!"*

And then she went into the bathroom to wash her hair and pincurl it with her new bobby pins.

After she left the room, my father looked at me and said, "Linda, when I was growing up, back on the frontier (my daddy always called his childhood home in the mountains of Virginia *the frontier*), we didn't set much store by giving birthday presents to adults. That was something done just for small young 'uns. And your momma's family, they were so poor, they didn't even do that much. But seeing how happy you've made your momma today has made me rethink this whole birthday issue. What I'm trying to say, Linda, is I believe you have set a precedent here."

And I did set a precedent. After that, my mother was showered with birthday presents every year: from my sister, from my brothers, from my father and from me. And, of course, the older we children got, the more money we made, and the nicer presents she received. By the time I was twenty-five, I had given her a stereo, a color television and a microwave oven (which she traded in for a vacuum cleaner).

For my mother's fiftieth birthday, my brothers and my sister and I pooled our resources and got her something spectacular: a ring set with a pearl surrounded by a cluster of diamonds. And when my oldest brother handed that ring to her at the party that

was given in her honor, she opened up the velvet gift box and peered at the ring inside. Then she smiled and turned the box around so that her guests could see her special gift, and she said, "Don't I have wonderful children?" Then she passed the ring around the room, and it was thrilling to hear the collective sigh that rippled through that room as the ring was passed from hand to hand.

After the guests were gone, I stayed to help clean up. I was doing the dishes in the kitchen when I overheard a conversation between my mother and father in the next room. "Well, Pauline," my father said, "that's a mighty pretty ring you've got there. I reckon that's about the best birthday present you've ever had."

My own eyes filled with tears when I heard her reply. "Ted," she said softly, "that's a might pretty ring and that's a fact. But the best birthday present I ever got? Well, that was a package of bobby pins."

Before becoming a mother I had a hundred
theories on how to bring up children.
Now I have seven children and only one theory;
love them, especially when they least deserve to be loved.
— Kate Samperi

HER PATH OF LOVE
Clare DeLong

ooking out through our kitchen window we can see a path from our porch through the grass to the property adjoining ours. That property belongs to my mother—that path also belongs to her.

Some time ago, I was involved in a near fatal car accident. With nine bones broken and other injuries, I needed constant care and my future recovery meant a possible stay in a rehabilitation center.

My husband decided a few days before my discharge to take me home. The doctor approved and the equipment that would be needed was shipped and set up in the spare bedroom. Wally and Mom had accepted the responsibility of caring for me twenty-four hours a day.

That's when her path began. It continued to be used every day. For the next two and a half months Mom traveled that path in sunshine, rain, snow, and sleet, during the morning and afternoon hours, even sometimes in the middle of the night.

I call it her path of love. The things she did for me at that time

are as many as the stars in the sky. She cared for me as only a mother could. Her love, tenderness, and gentleness shown to me will never be forgotten. Eighteen months later the path remains—a visible sign of a mother's love.

To love and be loved is to feel the sun from both sides.
— Barbara Johnson

ANNIE LEE'S GIFT
Glenda Smithers

Christmas had begun its countdown. At this time of the year Mrs. Stone admitted to only partial control of her students. It was amazing how such a lovely holiday could turn her well-disciplined students into spirited, noisy elves.

"Mrs. Stone, I spilled glue down my new pants," whined Chris.

"Mrs. Stone, my paper chain won't fit around the tree," complained Faye.

"Danielle is flicking paint everywhere!" squealed a girl from the sink area.

Where were her organized lessons and normal routine? And where was her peace of mind? They seemed to have taken a long recess. This recess, Mrs. Stone feared, would last until mid-January.

"Teacher?" A child's voice called from the activity table. Stepping over scraps of paper decorating the carpet, Mrs. Stone moved to where a few children were finishing their calendars for their parent's Christmas gifts.

"Yes, Annie Lee?" asked Mrs. Stone.

The little girl tossed back long, shining hair and answered politely. "Uh...if I finish my calendar, could I take it home

tonight? My mother wants to see it. She might have to go—"

"No, Annie Lee," responded Mrs. Stone automatically. "You may take it home on Friday like everybody else."

Annie Lee started to protest but the teacher moved quickly from the table, preoccupied with brushing silver glitter from her skirt.

The Little Drummer Boy's pa-rum-pa-pum-pum suddenly vibrated the room. "Lavenia, please turn off the record player!" To the rest of the class Mrs. Stone announced, "All right, boys and girls, it's time to clean up."

"Ahhh…." The expected groans of disappointment came and went.

At her desk, Mrs. Stone opened the lid to a small wooden chest and "Silent Night" was immediately recognized by the children. A quiet mood settled over the room as they listened.

"Shay, would you begin our show and tell today?" Mrs. Stone asked while closing the music box. The boy came to the front of the room and said with a slight boast, "I'm getting a red bike for Christmas."

Mrs. Stone closed her eyes. *Here we go again,* she thought. *"I want this and I want that."*

Annie Lee was next to share. Her long hair reflected the sunshine coming through the window as she came forward.

"My mother is sick and can't make the cookies for our party on Friday," she announced.

Mrs. Stone's eyes flew open. *I can't believe Mrs. Brown is using that same excuse,* she thought. *She couldn't attend PTA or parent-teacher conference for the same reason. Some parents just try to get out of their responsibilities.*

Annie Lee edged close to the teacher's desk and the music box. Her eyes sparkled as she spoke and one finger tenderly traced the Madonna and child painted on the lid. "When my mother gets well, she's going to buy me a music box exactly like yours, Mrs. Stone."

The teacher smiled and answered, "That's nice, Annie Lee, but it couldn't be *exactly* like mine. You see, this is very old. It was my great-grandmother's music box. Someday, I'll give it to one of my children."

The following day Annie Lee brought a thin strip of red velvet ribbon to the teacher's desk.

"Mother went to the hospital last night but she gave me this ribbon to wrap around the gift I made for her," she said.

"The ribbon is very pretty," said Mrs. Stone. Then she added, "I'm sorry your mother is in the hospital."

"Daddy said I could bring the calendar to the hospital if you—"

Annie Lee began her request again, but Mrs. Stone interrupted. "I've already told you that we will wrap them tomorrow and take them home on Friday."

Annie Lee looked disappointed. Her face brightened, however, when she remembered the gift she had for her teacher. "Mother made this for you!" she said happily and laid a red velvet bookmark in front of Mrs. Stone. Then she turned and skipped away. The teacher noticed that the sheen was missing from the little girl's hair that day; it was dull and tangled and uncombed.

Friday came. The Christmas tree, somewhat over-decorated, stood in the center of the room. Mrs. Stone wore the cranberry red dress she wore every Christmas and Valentine's Day. The children entered the room noisily, each aware that Christmas was near. But Annie Lee's chair was empty.

Feeling uneasy, Mrs. Stone sat down. She did not want to know the reason Annie Lee was not at school: one more burden added to twenty-five years of accumulated frustrations was more than she could bear.

As if in answer to her unspoken question, a student monitor entered the room and handed her a folded note. Trembling, she read the principal's hastily written note: "I thought you'd want to know. Annie Lee Brown's mother died early this morning."

Somehow Mrs. Stone managed to get through the day. When the party was over and the children had gone home to enjoy their holiday, Mrs. Stone stood alone in her classroom and cried. She cried for Annie Lee, for Annie Lee's mother, and for herself—and for the calendar that was intended to bring joy but didn't, and the red velvet bookmark so undeserved.

Mrs. Stone left the school very late that night. Stars twinkled in the sky above, lighting the way to Annie Lee's house. In her hands, Mrs. Stone carried the precious music box as if it were the Wisemen's treasure itself. She looked up at the brightest star and prayed the music box would help return Christmas to both their hearts.

A MOTHER'S SACRIFICE

I have been told that my mother, when she sur-
mised from the face of the physician that her
life and that of her child could not both be saved,
begged him to spare the child…. So through these
many years of mine, I have seldom thanked God for
His mercies without thanking Him for my mother.

James M. Ludlow

SPECIAL CHILDREN,
MINE AND GOD'S
Nancy Jo Sullivan
FROM *THE CATHOLIC DIGEST*

On a hot July morning, I awoke to the clicks of a broken fan blowing humid air across my face. That got me thinking about all the other things that had "broken down" in my life.

Parenting a daughter who has Down syndrome presents unique challenges. Although Sarah's heart surgery and many serious infections were over, now we faced catastrophic hospital bills. On top of that, my husband's job would be eliminated in just weeks, and losing our home seemed inevitable.

As I closed my eyes to try to put together a morning prayer, I felt a small hand nudge my arm. "Mommy," Sarah said, "I-I-I g-g-g-got r-r-ready for va-va-va-vacation Bi-Bi-Bible school all by myself!"

Next to the bed stood five-year-old Sarah, her eyes twinkling through thick, pink-framed glasses. Beaming with pride, she turned both palms up and exclaimed, "Ta-dah!"

I noticed her red-checked, seersucker shorts were on backward, with the drawstring stuck in the side waistband. A J. C. Penney price

tag hung from the front of a new, green polka-dot top, also on backward. She had chosen unmatched red and green winter socks to go with the outfit. Her tennis shoes were on the wrong feet, and she wore a baseball cap with the visor and emblem turned backward.

"I-I-I packed a b-b-backpack, t-t-too!" she stuttered, while unzipping her bag so I could see what was inside. Curious, I peered in at the treasures she had so carefully packed: five Lego blocks, a box of unopened paper clips, a fork, an undressed Cabbage Patch doll, three jigsaw puzzle pieces, and a crib sheet from the linen closet.

Gently lifting her chin until our eyes met, I said very slowly, "You look beautiful!"

"Thank y-y-you," Sarah smiled, as she began to twirl around like a ballerina.

Just then, the living room clock chimed 8:00, which meant I had 45 minutes to get myself, two toddlers, and a baby out the door.

As the morning minutes dissolved into urgent seconds, I realized I was not going to have time to change Sarah's outfit.

Buckling each child into a car seat, I tried to reason with Sarah. "Honey, I don't think you'll be needing your backpack for vacation Bible school. Why don't you let me keep it in the car for you?"

"No-o-o-o-o. I n-n-need it!"

And so I surrendered, telling myself her self-esteem was more important than what people might think of her knapsack full of useless stuff.

When we got to church, I attempted to redo Sarah's outfit with one hand while I held my baby in the other. But Sarah pulled away, reminding me of my early morning words, "No-o-o-o-o...I l-l-look b-b-beautiful!"

Overhearing our conversation, a young teacher joined us. "You *do* look beautiful!" the woman told Sarah. Then she took Sarah's hand and said to me, "You can pick up Sarah at 11:30. We'll take good care of her." As I watched them walk away, I knew Sarah was in good hands.

While Sarah was in school, I took the other two children and ran errands. All the while my thoughts raced with anxiety and disjointed prayer. What did the future hold? How would we provide for our three small children? Would we lose our home? These painful questions caused me to wonder if God loved us.

I got back to the church a few minutes early. A door to the sun-filled chapel had been propped open, and I could see the children seated inside in a semicircle listening to a Bible story.

Sarah, sitting with her back to me, was still clutching the canvas straps which secured her backpack. Her baseball cap, shorts, and shirt were still on backward.

Watching her from a distance, I became aware of warm emotion welling within. One thought rushed through my mind, one simple phrase: "I sure do love her."

Then, as I stood there, I heard that still, comforting voice that I have come to understand is God's—"That's the way I feel about *you*."

I closed my eyes and imagined my Creator looking at me from a distance: my life so much like Sarah's outfit—backward, unmatched, mixed up...

"Why are you holding that useless 'backpack' full of anxiety, doubt, and fear?" I could imagine God saying to me. "Let Me carry it."

I sensed that God was speaking not only to me, but to all those who struggle with lives that seem backward, inside-out, and out of control. We all want to be financially secure, free from illness, and immune to the inevitable pain that life brings. But God calls us to trust that what we need will be provided.

It is in these vulnerable times of weakness that we need to give our fear-filled backpack to the One who says, "You are precious in my eyes and I love you" (Isaiah 43:4).

That night as I once more turned on our crippled fan, I thanked God for the privilege of parenting Sarah. Through her, I realized, God had been revealed to me in a new way.

GOT A MINUTE?

David Jeremiah

A mother who had just finished reading a book on parenting…was convicted about some of the things she had been failing to do as a parent. Feeling this conviction, she went upstairs to talk to her son. When she got upstairs, all she could hear coming from her boy's room was the loud sound of his drums. She had a message she wanted to deliver, but when she knocked on the door, she got cold feet.

"Got a minute?" she said, as her son answered her knock.

"Mom, you know I always have a minute for you," said the boy.

"You know, son, I…I…I just love the way you play the drums."

He said, "You do? Well, thanks, Mom!"

She got up and started back downstairs. Halfway down, she realized that she had not conveyed the message she had intended so back she went to his door and once again knocked. "It's Mom again! Do you have another minute?" she said.

He said, "Mom, like I told you before, I always have a minute for you."

She went over and sat on the bed. "When I was here before I had something I wanted to tell you and I didn't get it said. What I

really meant to say was…your dad and I…we just really think you're great."

He said, "You and Dad?"

She said, "Yes, your Dad and I."

"Okay, Mom. Thanks a lot."

She left and was once again halfway down the stairs when she realized she had gotten closer to the message she intended but had still not told her boy that she loved him. So up the stairs again and back to the door again, and this time he heard her coming. Before she could ask he shouted, "Yeah, I have a minute!"

Mom sat down on the bed once more. "You know, son, I've tried this twice now and haven't gotten it out. What I really came up here to tell you is this. I love you. I love you with all my heart. Not Dad and I love you, but I love you."

He said, "Mom, that's great. I love you, too!" He gave her a great big hug.

She started out of the room and was back at the head of the stairs when her son stuck his head out of his room and said, "Mom, do you have a minute?"

She laughed and said, "Sure."

"Mom," he said, "did you just come back from a seminar?"

HER LOVE

No language can express the power and beauty and heroism and majesty of a mother's love. It shrinks not where man cowers, and grows stronger where man faints, and over the wastes of worldly fortune sends the radiance of its quenchless fidelity like a star in heaven.

E. H. Chapin

LOVE'S SACRIFICE
Kathi Kingma

*G*oing to an affluent high school wasn't easy. I watched with envy as many of the "rich" kids drove their parents' sports cars and bragged about where they *bought* their designer clothes. I knew there was never a chance for me to compete with their wealthy status, but I also knew that it was a near crime if you wore the same outfit twice in the same month.

Coming from a family of five, with a tight budget, allowed us little hope for style. That didn't stop me from badgering my parents that I needed more fashionable clothes. My mother would frown at me. "Do you *need* them?"

"Yes," I would say adamantly. "I need them."

So shopping we would go. My mom waited outside the dressing room while I tried on the nicest clothes we could afford. I can recall several of these "necessity trips." Mom always went without complaining, never trying anything on for herself, though she'd look.

One day, when I was at home, I tried on one of my new outfits and modeled it in front of my parents' full-length mirror. As I was deciding what shoes looked best with the outfit, my eyes

wandered to their closet, which was partially open. What I saw brought tears to my eyes. Three shirts hung on my mom's side of the closet. Three shirts that she'd worn endlessly and were old and faded. I pulled open the closet farther to see a few work shirts of my dad's that he'd worn for years. It had been ages since they bought anything for themselves, though their need was greater than mine.

That moment opened my eyes to see the sacrifices my parents had made over the years, sacrifices that showed me their love more powerfully than any words they could have said.

*Duty makes us do things well,
but love makes us do them beautifully.*
—*Phillips Brooks*

CHRISTMAS LOST & FOUND
Shirley Barkdale
FROM *MCCALL'S* MAGAZINE

We called him our Christmas Boy, because he came to us during that season of joy, when he was just six days old. Already his eyes twinkled more brightly than the lights on his first tree.

Later, as our family expanded, he made it clear that only he had the expertise to select and decorate the tree each year. He rushed the season, starting his gift list before we'd even finished the Thanksgiving turkey. He pressed us into singing carols, our croaky voices sounding more froglike than ever compared to his perfect pitch. He stirred us up, led us through a round of merry chaos.

Then, on his twenty-fourth Christmas, he left us as unexpectedly as he had come. A car accident on an icy Denver street, on his way home to his young wife and infant daughter. But first he had stopped by the family home to decorate our tree, a ritual he had never abandoned.

Without his invincible Yuletide spirit, we were like poorly trained dancers, unable to perform after the music had stopped. In our grief, his father and I sold our home, where memories clung to

every room. We moved to California, leaving behind our support system of friends and church. All the wrong moves.

It seemed I had come full circle, back to those early years when there had been just my parents and me. Christmas had always been a quiet, hurried affair, unlike the celebrations at my friends' homes, which were lively and peopled with rollicking relatives. I vowed then that someday I'd marry and have six children, and that at Christmas my house would vibrate with energy and love.

I found the man who shared my dream, but we had not reckoned on the surprise of infertility. Undaunted, we applied for adoption, ignoring gloomy prophecies that an adopted child would not be the same as "our own flesh and blood." Even then, hope did not run high; the waiting list was long. But against all odds, within a year he arrived and was ours. Then nature surprised us again, and in rapid succession we added two biological children to the family. Not as many as we had hoped for, but compared to my quiet childhood, three made an entirely satisfactory crowd.

Those friends were right about adopted children not being the same. He wasn't the least like the rest of us. Through his own unique heredity, he brought color into our lives with his gift of music, his irrepressible good cheer, his bossy wit. He made us look and behave better than we were.

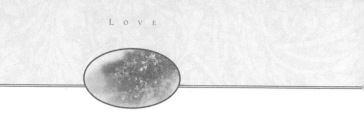

In the sixteen years that followed his death, time added chapters to our lives. His widow remarried and had a son; his daughter graduated from high school. His brother married and began his own Christmas traditions in another state. His sister, an artist, seemed fulfilled by her career. His father and I grew old enough to retire, and in Christmas of 1987 we decided to return to Denver. The call home was unclear; we knew only that we yearned for some indefinable connection, for something lost that had to be retrieved before time ran out.

We slid into Denver on the tail end of a blizzard. Blocked highways forced us through the city, past the Civic Center, ablaze with thousands of lights—a scene I was not ready to face. This same trek had been one of our Christmas Boy's favorite holiday traditions. He had been relentless in his insistence that we all pile into the car, its windows fogged over with our warm breath, its tires fighting for a grip in ice.

I looked away from the lights and fixed my gaze on the distant Rockies, where he had loved to go barreling up the mountainside in search of the perfect tree. Now in the foothills there was his grave— a grave I could not bear to visit.

Once we were settled in the small, boxy house, so different from the family home where we had orchestrated our lives, we hunkered down like two barn swallows who had missed the last

migration south. While I stood staring toward the snowcapped mountains one day, I heard the sudden screech of car brakes, then the impatient peal of the doorbell. There stood our grand-daughter, and in the gray-green eyes and impudent grin I saw the reflection of our Christmas Boy.

Behind her, lugging a large pine tree, came her mother, step-father, and nine-year-old half-brother. They swept past us in a flurry of laughter; they uncorked the sparkling cider and toasted our homecoming. Then they decorated the tree and piled gaily wrapped packages under the boughs.

"You'll recognize the ornaments," said my former daughter-in-law. "They were his. I saved them for you."

"I picked out most of the gifts, Grandma," said the nine-year-old, whom I hardly knew.

When I murmured, in remembered pain, that we hadn't had a tree for, well, sixteen years, our cheeky granddaughter said, "Then it's time to shape up!"

They left in a whirl, shoving one another out the door, but not before asking us to join them the next morning for church, then dinner at their home.

"Oh, we just can't," I began.

"You sure can," ordered our granddaughter, as bossy as her

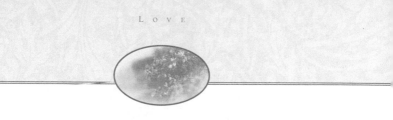

father had been. "I'm singing the solo, and I want to see you there."

"Bring earplugs," advised the nine-year-old.

We had long ago given up the poignant Christmas services, but now, under pressure, we sat rigid in the front pew, fighting back tears.

Then it was solo time. Our granddaughter swished (her father would have swaggered) to center stage, and the magnificent voice soared, clear and true, in perfect pitch. She sang "O Holy Night," which brought back bittersweet memories. In a rare emotional response, the congregation applauded in delight. How her father would have relished the moment!

We had been alerted that there would be a "whole mess of people" for dinner—but thirty-five? Assorted relatives filled every corner of the house; small children, noisy and exuberant, seemed to bounce off the walls. I could not sort out who belonged to whom, but it didn't matter. They all belonged to one another. They took us in, enfolded us in joyous camaraderie. We sang carols in loud, off-key voices, saved only by that amazing soprano.

Sometime after dinner, before the winter sunset, it occurred to me that a true family is not always one's own flesh and blood. It is a climate of the heart. Had it not been for our adopted son, we would not now be surrounded by caring strangers who would help us to hear the music again.

Later, not yet ready to give up the day, our granddaughter asked us to come along with her. "I'll drive," she said.

"There's a place I like to go." She jumped behind the wheel of the car and, with the confidence of a newly licensed driver, zoomed off toward the foothills.

Alongside the headstone rested a small, heart-shaped rock, slightly cracked, painted by our artist daughter. On its weathered surface she had written: "To my brother, with love." Across the crest of the grave lay a holly-bright Christmas wreath. Our number-two son admitted, when asked, that he sent one every year.

In the chilly but somehow comforting silence, we were not prepared for our unpredictable granddaughter's next move. Once more that day her voice, so like her father's, lifted in song, and the mountainside echoed the chorus of "Joy to the World," on and on into infinity.

When the last pure note had faded, I felt, for the first time since our son's death, a sense of peace, of the positive continuity of life, of renewed faith and hope. The real meaning of Christmas had been restored to us. Hallelujah!

Love is not blind; love sees a great deal more than the actual.
Love sees the ideas, the potential in us.
—*Oswald Chambers*

INSPIRATION

LAVENDER MEMORIES

Sandra Picklesimer Aldrich and Bobbie Valentine

FROM *HEARTPRINTS*

As Cotha Prior strolled past the new shop that sold body lotions and soaps, the lavender-wrapped bars displayed in the window caught her attention. Her daughter, Monica, would like those. Once inside, Cotha picked up the closest bar and held it to her nose. The fragrance carried her back to her childhood.

She remembered Margie, the little girl in her fifth grade class who always was poorly dressed and whose bathing habits were, well, not one of her regular habits. Even at that young age, Cotha knew how important the opinions of her friends were, so although she felt sorry for Margie, she couldn't risk being friends with her.

Then one afternoon, as the young Cotha colored the states on her homework worksheet, she casually mentioned Margie to her mother, who stopped in the middle of stirring the stew to ask, "What's her family like?"

Cotha didn't look up. "Oh, really poor, I guess," she answered.

"Well, it sounds as though she needs a friend," Mrs. Burnett said. "Why don't you invite her to spend Friday night with you?"

Cotha looked up quickly then. "You mean here? Spend the

night with me? But, Mom, she smells."

"Cotha Helen." Her mother's use of both names meant the situation was settled. There was nothing to do but invite Margie home. The next morning Cotha hesitantly whispered the invitation at the end of recess while her friends were hanging up their jackets and combing their hair. Margie looked suspicious, so Cotha added, "My mother said it's okay. Here's a note from my mother to give to yours."

So two days later they rode the school bus home while Cotha tried to ignore the surprised looks on her friends' faces as they saw the two of them together. Have two fifth grade girls ever been quieter? Cotha thought of other times when she'd been invited to spend the night with a friend. They would talk and giggle all the way to their stop.

Finally Cotha gave a determined little huff and said to Margie, "I've got a cat. She's going to have kittens."

Margie's eyes lit up. "Oh, I like cats." Then she frowned as though recalling a painful memory and added, "But my dad doesn't."

Cotha didn't know what to say then, so she feigned interest in something outside the school bus window.

Both girls were silent until the bus rolled to a stop in front of

the white house with the green shutters.

Mrs. Burnett was in the kitchen. She greeted Cotha and Margie warmly and then gestured toward the table set with two glasses of milk and banana bread. "Why don't you girls have a little snack while I tend to dinner," she said.

When the banana bread was finished, Mrs. Burnett handed each child identical paper-doll books and blunted scissors. Dressing the paper women in shiny dresses gave them something in common to talk about. By the time they washed their hands for dinner, they were chatting enthusiastically about school.

After the dishes were done, Mrs. Burnett said, "Time to take a bath before bed, girls." Then she held out scented soaps wrapped in lavender paper. "Since this is a special night, I thought you might like to use fancy soaps," she said. "Cotha, you first, and I'll wash your back for you."

Then it was Margie's turn. If she was nervous about having an adult bathe her, she didn't show it. As the tub filled, Mrs. Burnett poured in a double capful of her own guarded bubble bath. "Don't you just love bubble baths, Margie?" she asked as though the child bathed in such luxury every day.

She turned to pull Margie's grimy dress over her head, then said, "I'll look away as you take the other things off, but be careful

climbing into the tub. That brand of bubble bath makes it slippery."

Once Margie was settled into the warm water, Mrs. Burnett knelt down and soaped the wet washcloth heavily before rubbing it over the child's back.

"Oh, that feels good," was all Margie said.

Mrs. Burnett chatted about how quickly Cotha and Margie were growing and what lovely young women they were already. Repeatedly she soaped the washcloth and scrubbed Margie's gray skin until it shone pink.

Through the whole thing Cotha was thinking, Oh, how can she do that? Margie is so dirty. But Mrs. Burnett continued to scrub cheerfully, then washed Margie's hair several times. Once Margie was out of the tub, Mrs. Burnett dried her back and dusted her thin shoulders with scented talcum. Then, since Margie had brought no nightclothes, Mrs. Burnett pulled one of Cotha's clean nightgowns over Margie's now shining head.

After tucking both girls under quilts, Mrs. Burnett leaned over to gently kiss them good night. Margie beamed. As Mrs. Burnett whispered, "Good night, girls," and turned out the light, Margie pulled the clean sheets to her nose and breathed deeply. Then she fell asleep almost immediately.

Cotha was amazed that her new friend fell asleep so quickly;

she was used to talking and giggling for a long time with her other friends. To the sound of Margie's gentle breathing, Cotha stared at the shadows on the wall, thinking about all her mother had done. During Margie's bath, Mrs. Burnett had never once said anything to embarrass the girl, and she'd never even commented about how grimy the tub was afterward. She just scrubbed it out, quietly humming the whole time. Somehow Cotha knew her mother had washed more than Margie's dingy skin.

All these years later, the adult Cotha stood in the fragrant store, the lavender soap still in her hand, wondering where Margie was now. Margie had never mentioned Cotha's mother's ministrations, but Cotha had noticed a difference in the girl. Not only did Margie start coming to school clean and pleasant on the outside, but she had an inside sparkle that came, perhaps, from knowing someone cared. For the rest of the school year, Cotha and Margie played at recess and ate lunch together. When Margie's family moved at the end of the school year, Cotha never heard from her again, but she knew they had both been influenced by her mother's behavior.

Cotha smiled, then picked up a second bar of the lavender soap. She'd send that one to her mother, with a letter saying that she remembered what her mom had done all those years ago—not only for Margie but for Cotha as well.

GREAT LADY
Tim Hansel
FROM *HOLY SWEAT*

I remember when I was in fourth grade and you used to do things like stay up half the night just to make me a Zorro outfit for Halloween. I knew you were a good mom, but I didn't realize what a great lady you were.

I can remember your working two jobs sometimes and running the beauty shop in the front of our home so as to insure that our family would be able to make ends meet. You worked long, long hours and somehow managed to smile all the way through it. I knew you were a hard worker, but I didn't realize what a great lady you were.

I remember the night that I came to you late…in fact, it was near midnight or perhaps beyond, and told you that I was supposed to be a king in a play at school the next day. Somehow you rose to the occasion and created a king's purple robe with ermine on it (made of cotton and black markers). After all that work I still forgot to turn around in the play, so that no one really saw the completion of all your work. Still, you were able to laugh and love and enjoy even those kinds of moments. I knew then that you were a

mother like no other who could rise to any occasion, but I didn't realize what a great lady you were.

I remember when I split my head open for the sixth time in a row and you told the school, "He will be okay. Just give him a little rest. I'll come and check on him later." They knew and I knew that you were tough, but I didn't realize what a great lady you were.

I can remember in junior high and high school you helping me muddle through my homework—you making costumes for special events at school—you attending all my games. I knew at the time that you would try almost anything, if it would help one of your children, but I didn't realize what a great lady you were.

I remember bringing forty-three kids home at 3:30 one morning when I worked for Young Life and asking if it would be okay if they stayed over for the night and had breakfast. I remember you getting up at 4:30 to pull off this heroic feat. I knew at the time that you were a joyous and generous giver, but I didn't realize what a great lady you were.

I can remember you attending all my football and basketball games in high school and getting so excited that you hit the person in front of you with your pompons. I could even hear you rooting for me way out in the middle of the field. I knew then that you were one of the classic cheerleaders of all time, but I

didn't realize what a great lady you were.

I remember all the sacrifices you made so I could go to Stanford—the extra work you took on, the care packages you sent so regularly, the mail that reminded me that I wasn't in this all alone. I knew you were a great friend, but I didn't realize what a great lady you were.

I remember graduating from Stanford, and deciding to work for two hundred dollars a month loving kids through Young Life. Although you and Dad thought I had fallen off the end of the ladder you still encouraged me. In fact, I remember when you came down to help me fix up my little one-room abode. You added your special, loving touch to what would have been very simple quarters. I realized then—and time and time again—what a creative genius you were, but I didn't realize what a great lady you were.

Time wore on, I grew older and got married, and started a family. You became "NaNa" and cherished your new role, yet you never seemed to grow older. I realized then that God had carved out a special place in life when he made you, but I didn't realize what a great, great lady you were.

I got slowed down by an accident. Things got a little tougher for me. But you stood alongside as you always had. Some things, I thought, never change—and I was deeply grateful. I realized then

what I had known for a long time—what a great nurse you can be—but I didn't realize what a great, great lady you were.

I wrote some books, and people seemed to like them. You and Dad were so proud that sometimes you gave people copies of the books just to show what one of your kids had done. I realized then what a great promoter you were, but I didn't realize what a great, great lady you were.

Times have changed...seasons have passed, and one of the greatest men I have ever known has passed along as well. I can still remember you at the memorial service, standing tall and proud in a brilliant purple dress, reminding people, "How blessed we have been, and how thankful we are for 'a life well lived.'" In those moments I saw a woman who could stand tall and grateful amidst the most difficult of circumstances. I was beginning to discover what a great, great lady you are.

In the last year, when you have had to stand alone as never before, all of what I have observed and experienced all those years have come together in a brand new way. In spite of it all, now your laughter is richer, your strength is stronger, your love is deeper, and I am discovering in truth what a great, great lady you are.

Thanks for choosing me to be one of your sons.

ARE ALL THE CHILDREN IN?
Author unknown

I think of times as the night draws nigh
Of an old house on the hill,
Of a yard all wide and blossom-starred
Where the children played at will.
And when deep night at last came down,
Hushing the merry din,
Mother would look all around and ask,
"Are all the children in?"
'Tis many and many a year since then,
And the old house on the hill
No longer echoes childish feet
And the yard is still, so still.
But I see it all as the shadows creep,
And tho' many the years have been
Since then, I can hear my mother ask,
"Are all the children in?"
I wonder if, when those shadows fall
On the last short earthly day,

When we say good-bye to the world outside,
All tired of our childish play,
When we meet the Lover of boys and girls
Who died to save them from sin,
Will we hear Him ask as Mother did,
"Are all the children in?"

My mother used to look out the window
every morning and say,
"Maybe this will be the day when Christ comes again."
She lived with that daily anticipation....
It was my mother's hope until she went at last to be with him....
— B i l l y G r a h a m

MOTHER'S LEGACY

I shall never forget my mother for it was she who planted and nurtured the first seeds of good within me. She opened my heart to the impressions of nature; she awakened my understanding and extended my horizon, and her precepts exerted an everlasting influence upon the course of my life.

Immanuel Kant

BECAUSE

by Adria Dobkin

FROM HER VALEDICTORIAN SPEECH
MOUNTAIN VIEW HIGH SCHOOL

My mother started playing the cello when she was forty-six years old. She had always wanted to learn how to play, and finally, as a middle-aged mother of two teenagers, she decided to take lessons.

I listened to her scratch out "Twinkle Twinkle Little Star," and slowly progress to more challenging pieces. To say I wasn't her biggest fan is an understatement.

She would come to me with her frustrations, wanting to quit, and I wouldn't say anything. I wasn't very supportive.

It seemed to me a waste. Playing the cello wasn't something my mother could put on her college applications. She was never going to play with the London Symphony Orchestra. I didn't see the point.

But my mother's point was not to please admissions officers or wow her peers. She did it just because.

It's this strive for internal self-improvement that leads to a sort of glow. Knowing that you have done something special for no other reason but "because."

VIEW FROM MY WINDOW
Robin Jones Gunn
FROM *MOTHERING BY HEART*

I'm home from the hospital. What a harrowing week.
The tumor was benign. I am "repaired."
Dozens of ugly silver staples bind my flesh together.
Outside the trees are beginning to bud. The lawns are all green.
Fat pigeons strut on the roof of Sandra's yellow house.
A perky little squirrel keeps stopping by my second-story window.
He raises his paws and presses his nose to the glass.
He sits and watches, like a child peering
through the window of a toy store.
What does he see? The many bouquets?
The basket of cards from my well-wishing friends?
The whirling ceiling fan?
This pale woman propped up watching him?
Oh, here he is now! Hello, my furry friend.
He's scratching at the glass, looking this way and that.
On the phone lines behind him,
four pigeons perform their high wire act.
All they need are tiny parasols.

And maybe a roasted nut cart to entice my fluffy-tailed friend
to stop watching me and start watching them.
A jogger in a purple shirt huffs by,
startling the acrobats and sending
them across the street to Sandra's roof
where six of them now strut and coo.
It's a busy world out there. So very busy.
So full of life. In here?
I close my eyes to sleep. To quiet my soul. To heal.
Yes, the danger is passed. I am repaired.
And I shall never have another child.
At thirty-nine such news shouldn't shock me.
A friend said I should feel relieved.
But for so many years I've wondered if perhaps
there might be one more tiny life within me,
waiting to be born.
Now it's evident the answer is no.
What are you staring at, Mr. Squirrel?
Have you never seen a mother's tears?

WHAT REALLY MATTERS

One hundred years from now

It will not matter

What kind of car I drove

What kind of house I lived in,

How much money I had in my bank account,

Nor what my clothes looked like.

But one hundred years from now

The world may be a little better

Because I was important

In the life of a child.

W H E N   T H E   M O O N   D O E S N ' T   S H I N E
Ruth Senter

Usually the moon shines bright on clear May nights in eastern Pennsylvania. But tonight the moon is missing. All is dark. I notice brown circles under the lamp in the hall when Mother welcomes our 2:00 A.M. arrival from Illinois. I also notice brown circles under her eyes. Spots I'd never noticed before. Tired skin under gentle folds.

But here she stands, my mother of forty years. I sense an accumulation of nights waiting up for home-coming children, as though the years have cast shadows from the lamp onto her face. I see the years in the black and blue veins that have just this week felt the heart specialist's probe. I hear the years—like the ocean ringing in a seashell—in the doctor's diagnosis. "Red flag…enlarged heart…slow the pace…." I stare into uncertainty. Mother has been a steady pulse through the years. Tomorrow has been an assumed promise—a grand procession of family weddings, births, graduations, music recitals, ordinations, Christmas, Easter, Thanksgiving. Time has been an event, not a sequence.

As I look at Mother, I sense that someone has wound the clock. Time now has a cadence. Years have become increments. History

has a beginning and an end. I shiver in the early morning chill. But then Mother's arms wrap me in warmth, and I am home. A forty-year-old child reassured by her mother's touch. There is no time in touch. Welcoming arms know not the years.

I hear the teakettle whistling. Freshly baked chocolate chip cookies wait on the old ironstone plate that once served cookies from Grandma Hollinger's kitchen. Mother's chocolate chip cookies and Grandma Hollinger's ironstone plate pull me back into timelessness. We sip peppermint tea and laugh over a silly story Dad tells. Our laughter drowns out the clock. There is no time in laughter. Mother laughs the hardest of all. Dark circles. Tired circles of joy. Her children are home.

For a moment I forget bruised veins and ticking clocks. I am held together by things that do not change—a mother's early morning welcome, freshly baked chocolate chip cookies, an ironstone plate, peppermint tea, a mantel clock, and laughter. I am held together by a God who does not change. I know the God of time who is yet above time. I see tonight in my mother's face the strange paradox of time and timelessness. A rare glimpse of the divine.

I AM A MOTHER'S PRAYER

Author unknown

I am a mother's prayer: I am sometimes clothed in beautiful language that has been stitched together with the needles of love in the quiet chambers of the heart, and sometimes I am arrayed only in the halting phrases interrupted by tears which have been torn like living roots from the deep soil of human emotion. I am a frequent watcher of the night. I have often seen the dawn break over the hills and flood the valleys with light and the dew of the gardens has been shaken from my eyes as I waited and cried at the gates of God.

I am a mother's prayer: there is no language I cannot speak; and no barrier of race or color causes my feet to stumble. I am born before the child is born, and ere the day of deliverance comes, I have often stood at the altar of the Lord with the gift of an unborn life in my hands, blending my joyful and tearful voice with the prayers and tears of the father. I have rushed ahead of the nurse through the corridors of the hospital praying that the babe would be perfect, and I have sat dumb and mute in the presence of delight over a tiny bit of humanity, so overwhelmed I have been able to do

nothing but strike my fingers on the harps of gratitude and say, "Well, thank the Lord!"

I am a mother's prayer: I have watched over the cradle; I have sustained a whole household while we waited for a doctor to come. I have mixed medicine and held up a thermometer that read 104°. I have sighed with relief over the sweat in the little one's curls because the crisis was past. I have stood by a graveside and picked a few flowers to take home like old memories, and cast my arms around the promises of God to just hang on and wait until I could feel underneath me the everlasting arms.

I am a mother's prayer: I have walked and knelt in every room of the house; I have fondled the old Book, sat quietly at the kitchen table, and been hurled around the world to follow a boy who went to war. I have sought through hospitals and army camps and battlefield. I have dogged the steps of sons and daughters in college and university, in the big city looking for a job. I have been in strange places, for I have even gone down into honky-tonks and dens of sin, into night clubs and saloons and back alleys and along dark streets. I have ridden in automobiles and planes and ships seeking and sheltering and guiding and reminding and tugging and pulling toward home and heaven.

I am a mother's prayer: I have filled pantries with provision when the earthly provided was gone. I have sung songs in the night when there was nothing to sing about but the faithfulness of God. I have been pressed so close to the promises of the Word that the imprint of their truth is fragrant about me. I have lingered on the lips of the dying like a trembling melody echoed from heaven.

I am a mother's prayer: I am not unanswered, although mother may be gone, although the home may be dissolved into dust, although the little marker in the graveyard grows dim. I am still here: and as long as God is God, and truth is truth, and the promises of God are "yes and amen," I will continue to woo and win and strive and plead with boys and girls whose mothers are in Glory, but whose ambassador I have been appointed by the King Emmanuel. I am a mother's prayer....

*Measure wealth not by the things you have,
but by the things you have for
which you would not take money.*
— *Anonymous*

WOMAN OF EXCELLENCE

Her children stand and bless her;

so does her husband.

He praises her with these words:

"There are many fine women in the world,

but you are the best of them all!"

PROVERBS 31:28, 29

ACKNOWLEDGMENTS

A diligent search has been made to trace original ownership, and when necessary, permission to reprint has been obtained. If I have overlooked giving proper credit to anyone, please accept my apologies. If you will contact Multnomah Publishers, Inc., Post Office Box 1720, Sisters, Oregon 97759, correction will be made prior to additional printings. Please provide detailed information.

Acknowledgments are listed by story title in the order they appear in the book. For permission to reprint any of the stories please request permission from the original source listed below. We appreciate the authors, publishers, and agents who granted permission for reprinting these stories.

A TRIBUTE TO MOMS

"I Found You There" by Kathi Kingma. Used by permission of the author.

EARLY YEARS

"Alone Time for Mom" by Crystal Kirgiss. Used by permission of the author, a columnist for the *Detroit Lakes Tribune*, Minneapolis, MN, © 1996.

"Love Letter's to My Unborn Child" by Judith Hayes. Used by permission of the author. My "Love Letters" story came from the heart of a young mother to be. I had a very sad childhood, but I was determined from the start to express my love for my children. Sasha is now a pediatric R.N. and happily married.

GROWING UP

"What a Mother Says" by Robin Jones Gunn. Excerpted from *Mothering by Heart*, © 1996 Robin Jones Gunn. Used by permission of Multnomah Publishers, Inc., Sisters, OR.

"No More Oatmeal Kisses" by Erma Bombeck from *Forever, Erma* © 1996 by the Estate of Erma Bombeck. Used by permission of Andrew McMeel Publishing. All rights reserved.

"Seeing Each Other in a Different Light" by Susan Manegold, © 1998. Used by permission of the author. Originally printed in *Women's World* magazine.

LOVE

"Her Path of Love" by Clare DeLong, © 1996. Used by permission of the author. Clare has contributed articles for *Contents of the Weaker Vessel* and *Our Hope*, which are Christian newsletters; also *Christianity* magazine. Her home is in northern Illinois.

"Annie Lee's Gift" by Glenda Smithers, © 1997. Glenda Smithers is a preschool director, public speaker, and author of three children's missions books. She is a mom and grandmom in Kingsville, MO. Used by permission of the author.

"Special Children, Mine and God's" by Nancy Jo Sullivan. From *The Catholic Digest*, September 1993. © 1993 by Nancy Jo Sullivan. Used by permission of the author.

"Got a Minute?" by David Jeremiah. Excerpted from *The Power of Encouragement*, © 1997 by David Jeremiah. Used by permission of Multnomah Publishers, Inc., Sisters, OR.

"Love's Sacrifice" by Kathi Kingma. Used by permission of the author.

"Christmas Lost and Found" by Shirley Barkdale, © 1988. Originally appeared in *McCall's* magazine, December 1988. Used by permission of the author.

INSPIRATION